Ugly Duckling

RACHEL WEDDLE

UGLY DUCKLING

ISBN: 979-8-9880937-0-1

UGLY DUCKLING

DEDICATION

For my loving, supportive husband Dan, thank

you for loving me for me. My two sweet sons,

Lincoln & Henry. You two boys are my heart

& soul & I love you more than lips can tell.

This book is also dedicated to my inner child,

Little Rachel - I'm so proud of your strength.

UGLY DUCKLING

"When you try to prepare your child for a rough and tough world by being rough and tough with them, you simply become the first person in their life to bully them."

- Eli Harwood

Intro

"I HATE YOU!" I screamed as I ran down the hallway to my bedroom and slammed the door. I felt so much anger inside of me that I opened my door and yelled, "why can't you just die?!" I locked myself in my room and hid in my bed wishing I could disappear.

I was a sixteen-year-old girl living in a home with a controlling, alcoholic, abusive dad, so if you can imagine the fighting and yelling in our house was constant. My mother was the queen of giving silent treatment. So, when we weren't verbally or physically fighting, they were using emotional neglect to parent my brother and me.

By the time I was sixteen, I was fed up with my father's behavior and he hated it when I stood up to him. That is when things got really rough. My best friend at the time would call the fights in our home "World War III," because it would get scary. Anything that wasn't nailed down could and would turn into a weapon.

There were times I wanted to run away, hoping to get kidnapped or wished my parents dead because of the way they treated me. I was their only daughter and the youngest out of 5 kids. My parents both had children when they met and they decided to have my brother Anthony in hopes that he was a girl. When he wasn't, they tried once more and got me.

Living with Dad was like riding a roller

coaster that never stopped. Sober Dad and Inebriated Dad were like night and day. That is probably why I have no desire to ride on a roller coaster. I lived on one for the first 17 years of my life. Always living on edge in fight or flight; then there was the calm before the storm. As a child I learned very quickly how to read others' emotions in order to survive. I knew when I could relax and when it was time to walk on eggshells.

Mr. Bear

Some kids have their favorite blanket or doll, but I had Mr. Bear. He's an 18-inch brown teddy bear with a zipper compartment on his back. He used to have a battery-operated device in his back that would record what you say. I would hide my most valuable possessions in him, like my plastic rings and candy. He was my security item when I felt unsafe. When I needed to hide away in my room and cry, he was always there.

UGLY DUCKLING

I think he was a gift from my "Aunt Naomi" who is actually my dad's cousin. I received him as a gift around the age of two, when I had an accident on my grandma's wooden swing set. My brother was pushing an empty swing and I ran out in front of it and busted the right side of my forehead open. My dad had told me that they didn't take me to get stitches, just put a butterfly bandage on my head. I still have a small scar there to this day; I call it my Harry Potter scar.

Mr. Bear quickly became more than a stuffed animal, he was my comfort, my protector and was always there to chase away many nightmares. I slept with him every night and if I went to a friend's house for a sleepover, I brought Mr. Bear in my backpack. I remember once when I was seven or eight, I went to a sleepover and forgot him at home. I realized this as my mom was dropping me off and I started to panic. I don't know how I convinced her, but mom drove all the way home and back to bring him to me. That's probably the nicest thing she ever did for me.

Mr. Bear doesn't look like much now. He is an old bear now at approximately 36-year-old vintage bear. His black button eyes are scratched and the fabric around his nose is worn. His fur that was once soft and fluffy is now flat and rough. I can't bear the thought of him being put away in a box or storage bin somewhere, so I placed him on a shelf in Henry's room.

Recently, Henry has asked to start playing with him and taking his mid-day nap with Mr. Bear and it makes me extremely happy. I owe a lot to that tiny bear. He went through hell and back with me. Now he can be played with for many more years and be loved by my children.

Like a Bird

I absolutely loved my second-grade teacher.

Her name was Mrs. Applegate, and I thought

she was the nicest woman in the world. I felt so

lucky that I was in her class. She was so loving

and always had a smile on her face. I remember

my parents fighting a lot that year and the nurse

sent a letter home with concern because I

wasn't gaining weight.

UGLY DUCKLING

I was a very short, tiny girl. My mother would tell people that I "ate like a bird." Looking back, I think it was malnutrition and stress. I would eat meals then have horrible stomach aches. At bedtime I would sometimes have stomach aches. I had them so often at school that I had my own cot in the nurse's office so I could lay down after lunch. My stomach has always been my kryptonite.

One night I woke up and it was late, I heard the television on and knew dad was up. He was a late-nighter. He was sitting in his recliner in the dark, cigarette in hand. I told him I didn't feel good, and he offered to get me some warm milk. "That always helps," he told me.

My stomach aches just seemed to get worse, so they finally took me to the doctor.

The doctor told my parents I was too young for ulcers, so the diagnosis was a "nervous stomach." I was sent home with red cough syrup and was directed to take it any time I would have abdominal pain. My parents were instructed to stop feeding me a list of foods that would irritate my stomach.

I kept fighting for answers into my adulthood. In my twenties, I found out that I was lactose and gluten intolerant. That made me wonder if I had been slowly poisoning my gut my entire life. In the 80s and 90s, no one talked about gluten or food sensitivities. The doctor never mentioned that as a possibility to my parents. For that matter, he never questioned my parents about why I was such a "nervous" child. I have been on a gluten free diet for over 10 years now and I feel great. No

UGLY DUCKLING

daily stomach pain or nervous belly.

The New Kid

It's not clear what happened between my parents the summer before I started the 3rd grade, but it must have been pretty bad for us to move 2.5 hours north to live with my maternal grandparents. My half-brother Sean already lived with my grandparents and had since he was a kid. (My dad didn't want him to live with us, so my mom sent him to live with her parents. But that is not my story to tell).

Mom and I took over the back bedroom and my brother Anthony slept on the couch. Their little three-bedroom house was packed full. I didn't actually believe we were going to stay long, but when my mom told me she was enrolling us in school, and we were going to live with grandparents for a while I freaked out! I started crying telling her I missed home, that I missed my friends and I wanted to go back to my school.

At first, I assumed it was only temporary and when mom calmed down, we would just go back home. As weird as it sounds, I didn't feel safe being away from my dad. Being the new girl at a new school is very strange. I still have nightmares about that time in my life of feeling like such an outsider (sassenach, for my outlander friends) and extremely awkward. I was very shy and wouldn't talk to very many kids.

My brother would walk me to my class and hug me and tell me that if I needed him, he would be just down the hall in the 5th grade class. I think that was one of the few times we actually got along. I cried every morning before school, and he would try to comfort me. I hated that school and the stress from being the new girl made my stomach aches worse. My grandpa was so sweet and tried to make us happy by taking us grocery shopping for our favorite cereal. He let us pick the name brand cereal and not the generic bags. We came out of there with Captain Crunch, Cookie Crisp and Fruit Loops. But the expensive cereal didn't keep me from missing home.

UGLY DUCKLING

At the end of that first week of school I called my dad and begged him to make things right with Mom and say whatever she wanted to hear so we could come home. I told him I was miserable, and I refused to go back to school. He told me to give the phone to mom and he would take care of it. We went back home that Sunday, and by the next week I was enrolled in my old school again. I'd never been happier to see our little town.

My Imaginary Family

When I was around 9-10 years old I would daydream about living with another family, or about my "real parents" showing up and saving me. That is when I began to write poetry as a way to cope with my life. Once I showed my mom one of my poems that I planned to submit to a contest. I asked her if she wanted to read it. She didn't like it, and said it was disrespectful. The poem was about daydreaming about another land where I could live with another family and be happy. That was the first and last time I shared my poetry with her. along with poetry I also wrote in my diary. I still to this day journal about my life and feelings. I find it to be very therapeutic.

I needed my birth certificate for a school project around this time in elementary school. I asked mom if I could borrow it. She told me she lost my original birth certificate some time ago in our many moves, or maybe she lost it when we lived in a tent briefly when I was a toddler. She only had a copy, so I made up this story in my head that they must have stolen me, and my "real parents" still had the original certificate. I always wondered if my face was on a milk carton somewhere. I said it as a joke but deep down I really felt like I was in the wrong family.

UGLY DUCKLING

The majority of the time when I was stuck at home and not able to spend the night with friends, I would just lock myself in my room and drown out their fighting and chaos with my boom box. My bedroom was my original hiding place, my fortress of solitude and the only place I felt safe. During that time I had an imaginary twin sister named Nichole (my middle name) and we would play Barbies together and I would dance around and pretend to have concerts. I got lonely often since I wasn't close to my brother. My older brothers didn't live with us so when I was home it was just me and my Barbies and dolls.

We Moved Around a Lot

My parents were constantly moving us. I quickly became jealous and envious of my friends that had homes that they lived in for years and years. We stayed in the same small town but jumped from place to place all over the county. I never understood why we moved so much, but I never asked questions.

The different places we lived were

never really that nice - old trailers that had mice and cockroaches. A few times we rented houses, but I knew not to get attached because we would just end up back in a trailer. I always wanted a nice simple home with a stone sign in the front yard with our last name on it. I craved stability.

Finally, when I was 16 it felt like we made it out of poverty. Dad had a good job and somehow, he was approved for a loan to buy a home - a *real* home! Something I never had before. It was a 3-bedroom ranch-style home out in the countryside. We had a pond, a huge barn, and some land to call our own. Even through the chaos that was my life, I let myself be happy with this decision. I tried not to overthink it.

I felt like a normal kid for a second. I

wasn't embarrassed to have friends over. My bedroom wasn't just a hiding place but my sanctuary. I plastered my walls with posters of my favorite rappers and boy bands and there was no wood grain paneling behind those posters. I was proud of us! We made it a home - *but* it was short-lived like everything else.

My parents began to fight about money, and I overheard my dad say that their house payment was $1000 per month. In the year 2000 that was a lot of money for a house payment. I had to get out and I needed a plan.

I asked my best friend if I could move in with her family. She was like my sister. We grew up together. The first time I met her I was two or three years old and after that we were inseparable. Her parents agreed to let me live with them and I was so grateful! I packed up everything I needed, and I was gone.

The Haircut

I needed a haircut, and to save money Dad insisted on cutting my hair himself instead of taking me to a salon. I don't remember exactly how old I was at the time, but I was in elementary school. I remember looking in the mirror after he was done and being mortified! My hair was botched! The ends were chopped up and my bangs - oh my bangs - ended up way too short! I cried for days!

Dad felt so bad that he let me stay home

from school for a few days. After coming home from school that first day with my botched hair, he took off his hat and handed me the scissors and said, "do your worst." I was stunned.

"Huh?" I said.

"I need a haircut too and since I messed up your hair, you can chop up mine."

So that's exactly what I did. Kitchen scissors in hand, I butchered my dad's hair like I was pruning a chia pet. At that moment, it did make me feel better. After that he was never allowed to cut my hair again. Mom made sure to take me to a salon.

Dr. Jekyll and Mr. Hyde

My dad had a huge imagination, and he was a big dreamer. He was very much a mad scientist, and I loved that about him. He believed that one day the world would have hydrogen cars, he also believed in aliens and all things Area 51. He was always making up recipes or writing down experiments and inventions.

When my dad was sober, he was the best dad, my white knight. He Had a great sense of humor. He loved to watch John Wayne & Indiana Jones Movies. I loved watching Saturday morning cartoons with him as a kid. A few of our favorites were x-men, The gummy Bears, and Duck Tales. Sometimes I think he liked the cartoons more than we did.

My sophomore year in high school was rough and he could tell even though I don't remember him ever asking me if I was okay, he had a dozen roses delivered to the front office for me. He signed the card: "Guess who loves you?"

But I always knew those sweet moments and kind gestures would never last. I know he struggled with his self-worth. He always saw himself as the black sheep of his own family. He had a hard childhood growing up with his father. My Grandpa Roach was verbally and physically abusive. I know now that dad did the best he could with what he had while struggling with his demons.

Drunk dad, he was this angry stranger. Always belittling me, calling me names, telling me I was boring and that he wasn't impressed by me. That really affected my self-esteem. It made me feel ugly and unworthy.

He liked to pick fights and he loved to argue. It was very much a love/hate relationship. I tried my best to stay in my room and out of the way. I could always feel the tension in the house even before he spoke.

The older I got, the more I realized that his behavior was wrong and unacceptable. I couldn't stay quiet any longer. When I was 15 or 16 years old is when we really started butting heads. I had found my voice and I made sure he knew that the way he was treating us was wrong and I refused to put up with it any longer.

Whenever he was disrespectful or abusive to my mother, I would jump in to take the focus off of her. Of course, that would make him furious. I think he even drank more when my brother and I would step in. I didn't know at the time that I was an Empath, and I was taking on the negative energy. I would act out of character and say and do horrible things to him. He taught me how to be passive aggressive and how to argue at a pro-level.

I have dodged glass ashtrays, remotes, even our wall telephone got thrown down the hallway at me several times. I would scream at him that I wished he were dead. We would all slam doors and go to our corners of the house.

Our family motto should have been "always go to bed angry."

Then the next morning, Sober Dad would be back and act like nothing happened. It was very confusing especially when I was little. It made me feel like I was responsible for his emotions and behavior. Now as an adult I know that is not true and I try so hard not to let my mood affect my children. But if I notice that they are in a bad mood I do try to cheer them up. My goal is for them to be their happiest, healthiest selves so they can thrive.

Coping

Dark humor and sarcasm became my coping mechanism through those rough years as a child. I thought if I could make jokes about the things, I went through then it wasn't that serious. I don't remember feeling the need to tell a teacher or counselor at school because for a while I thought everything was normal.

My first-grade teacher had a sit down meeting with my parents. She told them that I daydreamed too much, and she felt like I should repeat the first grade over again. Since starting my healing journey, I think I was disassociating because of the trauma I was experiencing, but from the outside it looked like daydreaming. Being held back a grade that young always stayed with me. I felt dumb, I wished the teacher would have dug a little deeper into why I was behaving that way.

I definitely had self-destructive behavior in my teen years but luckily for me I wasn't dumb and knew when to "take a chill pill," as my dad would say. Whether it was my guardian angel or the Universe looking out for me, I always knew I was going to be okay.

Storyteller Dad

Carl Roach was the biggest bullshitter I've ever known. I never knew if he was telling the truth or not when he got in a storytelling mood. He went into the Marine Corp right out of high school. I think that was to get away from his dad. But he was only active for a few short years then was discharged.

Once Dad told me that he and a few other guys went AWOL so they could go to

Woodstock and got caught. Then he said he was stationed in Hawaii and got mixed up with a cartel and had to rat them out to get an honorable discharge from the military. I would just laugh and say, "ok Dad, sure" and then move on.

When I started asking questions about our family history, he had all kinds of answers. He always said we were Irish and that our ancestors had a castle in Ireland. Then we were related to the famous Billy the Kid. I always hoped we had famous or noble ancestors but never knew for sure.

My grandma Jones was the genealogist of the family. Turns out we are not only Irish but Scottish through my paternal great-grandfather. Thanks to my grandma's research in the 1990s, she gave me a book a few years ago with all the information dating back to the 1700s when our bloodline stepped foot onto American soil from Scotland. I'm guessing Dad never talked to her about the book she made.

Dad always played the black sheep card and that it was him against his family. Funny because I always felt it was me against my family. We didn't see his side of the family very often because of that. But I never got that vibe from them. I loved spending time with my aunts and uncles and playing with my cousins. I still ask myself what made him feel like an outsider. I feel like the outsider of my family but because I'm trying to break generational curses and work through my trauma. I refuse to accept that I'm damaged and just give in. I want to prove that your past or your upbringing doesn't define you.

Pancakes

Some nights I would keep my door locked while I slept. On good nights I'd keep it open, but those were few and far between. One morning I woke up very early to the smell that made my mouth water. I was scared to get out of bed. The night before, Dad went on a drunken rampage - yelling, throwing things around the house, and hitting Mom.

I gripped Mr. Bear tightly, decided to be brave and get up. I listened at my bedroom door for a moment for any movement outside. Hearing nothing alarming, I unlocked my door and stuck my head out. My bedroom was down a short hallway just off the kitchen in our trailer.

Dad turned when he heard me and said cheerfully, "Good morning, Honey! I made pancakes!"

I knew the alcohol had left his system and we would have a few good hours. I loved my dad SO much more when he was sober but even at a young age, I knew that it was only temporary. He drank daily as if it were water.

In our house, pancakes had two meanings: celebrating that it was the weekend, but the pancakes were also Dad's peace offering for whatever awful thing he said or did that week. He put his love and apology into our breakfasts. He would have my brother and I guess what the secret ingredient was that day.

Examples were banana, apple, cinnamon, or chocolate chip. I loved this game and I loved when he made pancakes because it made me feel like we were a normal family.

Then we would all watch Saturday morning cartoons together. Sunday mornings were also special to me. Dad would make biscuits and gravy and those are my absolute favorite meal. If we had extra money that week, he would take all four of us to our favorite local restaurant, Chambers Smorgasbord.

I still love pancakes and B&Gs as an adult, but now that I must be gluten free, B&G's have turned into a special treat. My husband makes them from scratch for me on special occasions like Mother's Day and my birthday. In our household, we make pancakes with our kids to bond with them. Henry is two and loves to help in the kitchen. Anytime he

asks for pancakes we make them. So I hope one

day when the boys are older and they think

back to when mom and dad made pancakes

with them I hope it makes them smile.

Cigarettes & Beer

Smoking tobacco, marijuana, and drinking beer were dad's three favorite hobbies. He smoked tobacco like a chimney, and I often worried about his health. Hell, I worried about my own health in the smoky haze of my childhood. At the young age of 9 or 10 years old I was very aware of how often my dad smoked cigarettes, and wondered how something that smelled so bad could be good for you.

I hated the smell of second-hand smoke. When I left the house, the smell of smoke was noticeable on my clothing. My clothes would stink, and sometimes they looked dingy. Kids at school would make comments and make fun of me. I was so embarrassed that I would spend a lot more time in my room with my bedroom door shut, packing the bottom of my door with towels and blankets to keep out the smell. On top of that, I would use *so much* body spray. Bath & Body Works Cucumber Melon was my favorite at that time. Anything vanilla-scented was also great at masking the cigarette smell.

Dad smoked everywhere, that included the house and in the car. I remember asking him once if he would roll his window down more than half an inch while we were riding in our minivan. In the late 90's the windows in the back of the minivan didn't roll down or open. He got very angry and snapped, "UNTIL YOU

PAY THE BILLS YOU DON'T TELL ME
WHAT TO DO!" My heart was crushed, he
didn't care that I was coughing and that the
smoke bothered me. I sank back in my seat and
kept my mouth shut the rest of the ride. I
honestly believe that 17 years of breathing
second-hand smoke is why I have a chronic
cough.

Not long after that, I brought up a math
project that we had been working on regarding
family savings. The teacher helped me
calculate the amount of money he was spending
on cigarettes per year and asked him if he
wanted to know how much money we would
save if he quit smoking. In fact, Dad didn't
want to know that information - and he
grounded me for being a smart ass.

After that I realized I was just wasting

my energy. He would never stop smoking. I tried smoking as a pre-teen because I wanted to look cool, but I hated it.

However, marijuana was Dad's true favorite. He was a product of the 60s & 70s, so of course he loved to smoke weed. He told me that when he switched from Catholic to public high school, everyone called him Roach Clip. It was no big deal for dad to have a pot plant or two growing in his closet during my childhood.

I'm sure your parents had the "don't do drugs" talk with you, right?? Mine didn't. Dad would say, "Rachel, marijuana is a gift from the earth. It has been around for thousands of years and it's not bad. When you are older you can try it."

I liked the smell of marijuana and tried it several times as a teenager. Growing up in a town with a population of approx. 2,000 people there wasn't much to do. There was always a joke that you either partied or got pregnant. I liked being a party girl.

Nosing under my parent's bed one day, I found Dad's stash box. It was a small metal tin with all his supplies which usually included: rolling papers, weed, and his pipe. I would get into it often after that day and steal his roaches. He finally realized that someone had found his stash and left a note inside his box for the thief that said: *STAY THE FUCK OUT!*

That was the last time I got into Dad's stash. I started getting weed from my friends instead. The next time I got into his stash was after his death. I wanted to smoke it but my mom decided to flush it down the toilet. I never asked her why she did that.

His beer of choice was Miller Genuine Draft, he would drink a case of MGD every other day. When I was young, I remember him cracking open a beer as soon as he got home. Then he started taking it with him to work in a cooler, and he would drink it on his way home too. Looking back at all the jobs he jumped from, I now understand that his drinking played a big factor in that.

If you saw my dad out with a thermos-type cup, there was a 90% chance it had cold beer in it. Dad would start the day by drinking coffee, occasional glass of sweet tea, but then would switch over to beer in the afternoon to evening. I never saw him drink a glass of water.

He had built up such a tolerance to beer over the years that it didn't seem to affect him - it only made him mean. He even had that dark reddish tint to his skin. If you have a close friend or family member that is an alcoholic, you know what I'm talking about.

I only ever saw him stumble one time down the hallway of our countryside house one time. It was after a cookout/party my parents threw at our house. You know, the sort of get-together where the adults want to drink and they bring their kids, but then ignore their kids the whole time. Someone at that party brought their infant and my friend and I volunteered to watch her. There were multiple smells floating around that party. I'm sure there was more going on than just beer and marijuana, but we mostly stayed in the house away from the festivities.

After the party started to fizzle out, Dad came in and tripped over his own feet and went down in the hallway, crashing like a ton of

bricks. I've never laughed so hard in my life. In

between the laughs I asked if he was alright,

and he gave a thumbs up and got himself up

and the rest of the way to his bed.

Theme Park Dad

Dad was a kid at heart, he loved to have fun,
when he allowed himself to. The first theme
park I have memory of is Kings Island. I had to
be around five or six when we took that trip. I
recall mom waking me up really early in the
morning, we loaded up the station wagon and
then I got in the car and went back to sleep. It
felt like we drove for ever but Mason, Ohio
was only about three hours away.

I remember we arrived before the park opened, so we stayed in the car. My brother and I got bored and hungry quickly. I asked if we could get breakfast, but mom and dad said no, we had a cooler full of food and snacks to save money. I think I had a bologna sandwich and chips for breakfast.

The only things I can remember about the rest of that day were my pretty pink pants and top I was wearing, and that we got to take home a souvenir Kings Island photo keychain. We also took a few trips in my childhood to Holiday World in Santa Claus, Indiana.

The Kentucky Kingdom trip when I was maybe 14 was really fun. My brother and I were allowed to bring a friend with us. That never happened because my dad hated feeding and paying for our friends to do activities with us. But not this time, so my best friend Liza and I ran around riding the huge ferris wheel, chasing boys, giving the cute ones our phone number. We thought we were hot shit because we were from a different state. You know, typical teenage girl stuff - stopping to pose with our disposable camera and take a selfie way before it was called a selfie.

Kentucky Kingdom was the last theme park we went to, and then we didn't take another family trip until I was 16. I didn't know it at the time, but it would be our last family vacation together.

Bumper Sticker Quote Dad

Dad loved to throw quotes at us so much, it sounded like he spoke in bumper stickers. His two favorites were "you bore me," and "wish in one hand, and spit in the other." Who says things like that to their children?! Another one I remember him saying was "life sucks and then you die."

Some of the quotes he used to say stick with me and pop up in my head when I'm triggered or feeling depressed. I've been told that it has a name. It's called Complex PTSD and it stems from chronic or long-term exposure to trauma. When I learned about this term and researched it, it makes so much sense and explains a lot of my behavior.

He also liked to use quotes from his favorite shows. When something good happened, he would say "I love it when a plan comes together" - that one was from the A-Team. He also quoted John Wayne often. He often told me "Treat others how you want to be treated," so when he was being abusive I made sure to throw that in his face. He was definitely a "rules for thee, not for me" kind of guy.

Revenge

To get back at my dad after a few bad fights,

my friend and I took some white paint and a

couple paint brushes down the road and painted

C.R. sucks in huge letters on the two iron

bridges by my house. My dad drove across

these bridges frequently so I knew he would

see the graffiti. A few days later he approached

me in the kitchen and said, "I bet you think

you're real cute huh?" I acted like I had no idea

what he was talking about and denied it.

"I saw your handy work on the bridge. Don't

worry - I won't forget that."

I was so proud of myself for keeping my cool

and for being brave enough for my passive-aggressive behavior. He taught me well.

When my parents would leave my brother and I home alone I would sip a little bit of my mom's wine, then replace it with water. She liked to drink jugs of David Mogan red wine, I thought it tasted like juice. Sometimes I would just dump a portion of it out and fill it with water just to spite her.

Another time after one of our fights I threw pieces of bologna on top of dad's truck roof. I heard a kid at school say that it would eat the paint, but it didn't do anything to it.

The Limo

"Hey dad, the spring dance is coming up. Can you rent a limo for me and my friends?"

I couldn't believe I had the courage to ask him, but I knew that if I could catch Dad on a good day, I could get my way. Plus, my dad liked to show off. So, if he could afford it, he would do it.

I was an 8th grader, and this dance was a big deal to me. I heard some other kids were getting limos and I wanted to fit in for once.

The planets aligned and Dad rented a limo for me. I felt like a princess that day. I asked 3 or 4 friends to ride with me. We all met at my grandma's house just outside of town. I wore a semi-formal spaghetti strap dress that mom bought me from DEB in the mall. It was red with black lace over the top. We asked the limo driver to make a few laps around town before he dropped us off at the dance. I didn't want the night to end. It was the first time in a long while I felt like a normal kid. I was happy that night and I felt beautiful.

Bullied

Most of the time, I hated school. I was an easy target for the kids at school to tease me. My last name was Roach. I had an awful underbite with crooked teeth. I was short and very petite. The names kids would call me sent me home many times crying. The kids were so cruel.

I never felt like I fit in with my classmates. My best friend was in the grade below me, and I just wanted to be with her all day. I do remember having a few friends from all different groups over the years. I tried to be friends with everyone. When the 5th grade rolled around, I was beginning to feel like I was finding my place. I was playing softball, and I was friends with several popular girls.

Then a guy in my class spread a rumor that I had been saying terrible things about my friends that were popular. Instead of asking me about it, all those "friends" just ghosted me. I was crushed. Then came middle school and I just tried to be invisible, but the bullies never stopped. By the time I got to high school I had very few close friends.

My childhood bestie started homeschooling after middle school, so I didn't have her during the day to help me feel brave. The high school girls got so mean I would avoid certain hallways and felt safest hanging out with a group of redneck boys. They were less dramatic and made me laugh. I dated a few of them but the majority of them were like brothers to me.

Of course, because I was a girl hanging out with a group of guys in high school, I was instantly deemed a "whore." There was no winning with my peers. I skipped lots of days in high school. The anxiety of getting picked on was too much. Some days my stomach felt like it was inside out.

By the end of my junior year, I reached my limit. The school drama plus the lack of support from my parents became too much. I dropped out my senior year. I spent that time drinking and partying to forget my troubles. It worked for a while until my boyfriend, who is now my husband, sat me down and said, "Hey I love you and I don't want you to not finish high school. Please get your GED."

I went to a few adult education classes to practice for the test. After one failed attempt, I passed. I was so glad to get that done and over with, so I could move on with my life.

Myrtle Beach

When I was 16, Dad scrapped enough money together to take us to Myrtle Beach, South Carolina. I had never seen the ocean and I was so excited. I asked if I could bring a friend and of course that was asking too much. "This is supposed to be a family vacation, I'm not paying for one of your friends." My brother also got shot down when he asked if he could bring a friend, too.

UGLY DUCKLING

The road trip was long but not horrible, from our house to Myrtle Beach was 12 hours straight through, but it took us about 16 hours altogether with all our stops. Once we got to our hotel, nothing else mattered. I could pretend to be someone else, and we could act like we were a happy loving normal family.

It was nice to see my parents relax. Walks on the beach, Dad fishing off the pier (he loved to fish). I was allowed to make a long-distance call to my best friend and tell her all about the trip so far. I missed her so much!

One evening as the sun was going down on the beach, I exhaled and felt my whole body relax for the first time ever. I couldn't believe how peaceful and happy the beach made me. I made friends with a group of kids that were my age, a handful of boys from

Hazzard, Kentucky, and then two girls from North Carolina. We had a blast together. I exchanged phone numbers with the girls and one of the guys but we didn't stay in touch. Seeing my parents in vacation mode was like seeing a different side of them. I think they relaxed as well. When it was time to start our trek home, I was angry of course. I didn't want to go back to Indiana. I wanted to stay at the beach for the rest of my life. The first rest stop we came to I seriously considered running off or just staying in the bathroom stall and hoped that they would forget me. Sadly, mom came looking for me and told me to hurry up.

When I got back home, I showed off my tan to my two best friends and the cute shorts I brought home. They were teal and had writing on the butt that said "booty or juicy" at the time

I thought I was hot shit. We never took another family vacation after that, and the next year is when I moved out.

I do think that trip planted a travel bug in me though. I love flying and I want to visit all 50 states. I have traveled to 20 so far and I can also check Canada and Belize off my list. I want to see as much of the world as I can while I can.

Boys & Booze

From as far back as I can remember I have

been boy crazy. My diary from elementary

school days was filled with names of boys I

liked or who I thought were cute that week. I

was a hopeless romantic from the start.

Looking back, the older I got the more attention

I wanted from boys. I'm sure it had everything

to do with not getting the attention I needed at

home. I yearned for a boy to tell me I was

pretty and that he loved me, because I felt that I was ugly. I felt that way my entire childhood. I was a tomboy that also played with barbies.

There were a few times as a teenager I put myself in a few sketchy situations but I was fearless. I didn't care one bit. When I was a sophomore, a boy in a yellow Camaro caught my attention.

I was running errands with my mom one Saturday afternoon in our small town. Each group of kids had a certain spot where they would park and hangout. We drove past a church parking lot in the middle of town and there sat the yellow Camaro. I quickly asked mom to pull into the church, I wanted to stay in town and hangout with this guy. She asked me if I knew the boy and I told her yes, but I didn't know him that well. I just knew he lived near me.

I had 10 seconds of bravery, walked up to him, said "Hey so you wanna drive me home later" he smiled and said "sure." I waved a hand to my mom letting her know I was good, and she left. She never asked any other questions. After that I wasn't afraid to let a guy know I liked him.

I had lots of guy friends because guys were easier to be around. I dated several guys after the yellow Camaro guy. I started going to parties every weekend. My schedule was school, then work for a few hours, then party on repeat. My underage alcoholic beverage of choice was Smirnoff Ice or Boone's Farm.

Drinking was such a fun outlet for me. I wasn't a mean drunk like my dad. It made me happy and clouded my thoughts and I could relax. It felt amazing not to be walking on eggshells and hurting. I was carefree for the first time and I was going to hold on to that as long as I could.

By the time my 21st birthday rolled around, I was already a seasoned party girl. I didn't even go to a bar and celebrate. Just a quick stop at the liquor store and home to my apartment. My twenties were all about fun and compartmentalizing my trauma. I didn't even have to think about it. I was skilled at burying my feelings about my family. I would get with a guy, have my fun, he would hurt me, then I'd move on to the next.

If I could go back and tell her anything during my teen years, it would be that she is worthy without a guy's approval. I'd tell her to love herself first, and not to worry what other people think of her.

The Time He Shot My Tire

It was a Saturday. I was 16 years old and the last place I wanted to be was at home.

"Dad, do you care if I drive over to Sam's house?" I asked while not making eye contact.

"NO," he said firmly.

"What?! Why??!" I exclaimed.

"I said *no*." He said firmly.

As I stood there expecting more of an explanation, I could feel the rage building up inside me. *What the fuck is wrong with him? I* asked myself. As I turned to leave, I mumbled

under my breath: "well, *I'm going anyway.*"
From behind me I heard him roar "the hell you
are!"

Dad was a control freak. He loved to be
dictator of the house. The older I got, the less
he could control me and he hated it. Teenage
Rachel was not the meek and obedient type. I
am my father's daughter so I pushed back hard.
I stomped my way to the kitchen to use the
phone. I was determined to leave.

As I was dialing Sam's phone number, I
heard Dad coming down the hall. Just as Sam
picked up, he grabbed the phone from me, and
my instincts told me to *run*. I headed as fast as I
could down the hallway to my room and just as
I reached my bedroom door, I heard the phone
hit the wall behind me.

I locked my door and threw myself

against it. After I thought things had settled down, I opened my door. But Dad was waiting for me to come out. Holding his .22-gauge shotgun, he headed outside. I had no idea what he was doing until I heard the first shot ring out from the driveway.

I ran outside and screamed "you bastard!" He had shot the back passenger tire of my Chevy Beretta.

"Try to leave now" he said, smiling as he walked back inside. I stood there for a few moments in disbelief, thinking about my next move. My dad and I were toxically competitive like that. We fought over getting the last word or action so our fights could and would go on for days.

I grabbed my purse and began to walk down the road. If I couldn't drive to my friends,

I would just walk there. It was only a few miles away. After about 10-15 minutes of walking, I heard a car coming and turned to see my mom. She made me get in the car and she took me the rest of the way to my friend's house.

I slept over at my friend's house for several nights after that incident to hide out. I was forced to ride the school bus to school that week because my car had a flat tire, and I didn't know when I would make the money to fix it. At the end of the week, to my surprise dad paid to get me a new tire but never apologized for the fight or for his insane behavior.

Thanksgiving

Getting my first serious boyfriend at 17 helped distract me and I was able to spend more time outside my house. Thanksgiving of 2002 I had decided I was going to my boyfriend's family dinner. I can laugh about this story now, but that day was not fun.

I woke up that morning to the sky spitting snow. I slept in late and remember hearing my parents getting ready to leave. They were headed to Indianapolis to spend the day with Aunt Naomi and Aunt Tonya (my dad's cousin and her partner). My brother Anthony was going with them, so I was about to have the whole house to myself. I was excited to turn on some music, get something to eat and then spend two or three peaceful hours doing my hair and makeup before I met up with my boyfriend.

After I got ready, I needed to get something out of my car, but I can't recall what I needed. I was just going to run outside quickly, so not thinking anything of it, I didn't grab a jacket. When I got to my passenger door it was locked, so I ran around to the driver's door only to find it locked as well. I needed to get my keys, so I wasted no time getting back up to the kitchen door.

As I reached for the kitchen doorknob, I thought for a split second *"what if I got locked out?"* As I turned the knob, it didn't move.

74

FUCK!! No, this can't be happening! I thought.
I tried turning the knob and it was definitely
locked. My heart sank and I started to panic.
What was I going to do?

My mind started to race, and I felt tears
welling up in my eyes. I couldn't cry too much
because it was so cold out, my tears would
freeze. My parents were 2 hours away, it's
freezing cold, I don't have a coat on, it's
snowing. I can't call for help because my cell
phone was in the house and we have no close
neighbors because we live in BUMFUCK,
EGYPT! I ran around the house and checked
the back door, no luck there. Then I checked to
see if all the windows were locked; they were.
The only window that wasn't locked was the
crank out window above the kitchen sink.

I quickly came up with a plan. I ran to

the garage, luckily it wasn't locked. I grabbed a
bucket to stand on and a garden shovel to pry
the window open. After a few minutes it
actually worked. I was able to pry it open
enough for my body to fit. For once I was
thankful that I was only 90 lbs. because it was a
tight squeeze. I shimmed up into the window.
As I did that, I realized the kitchen sink was
full of dirty water so I had to be careful not to
fall in it. When my legs were the only thing
sticking out of the window, I said to myself out
loud: "wouldn't it be funny if someone drove
by at this moment and saw my legs hanging out
of the window? Then I would get help."

Once my whole body was in the house I
collapsed to the floor. "I can't believe I fucking
did that!" I shouted out loud. That whole
process felt like it took hours, I glanced at the

clock, and it had only been about 45 minutes. I was so impressed and proud of myself.

I was filthy and needed to change my clothes and head to Thanksgiving dinner with my boyfriend. I tried to close the window, but prying open the window stripped the crank so it wouldn't close all the way. I didn't have time to mess with it, so I closed it up the best I could and decided to deal with it later.

My adrenaline was pumping, and I didn't really calm down until I got to my boyfriend's house. That evening when I got home my parents were waiting with questions about the window. I think their first thought was that someone tried breaking in while I was gone. Cold air was pouring in, and they wanted to know what happened. I explained everything to them and stupid me I actually expected them to say, "we are so glad you're okay." That was not the case.

They were both equally furious that I broke the window. And I was expected to pay them to fix it. I didn't care about the window. I was so upset that they weren't concerned about my wellbeing, and the fact that *I was scared of freezing to death with no way of getting help at the time.* Anytime they brought it up to throw it in my face, I would ask, "what was I supposed to do?" Dad would never answer me. My hate for them really started to sink into my bones after that.

Then I started to ask myself "the whys"- *why is this happening to me, why do they treat me so badly, why me?* I hated my life at home.

I didn't live there much longer after that, the tension and fighting only got worse until I had enough. I moved in with my childhood best friend and her family. But because my dad was a control freak and I wasn't 18 yet, I wasn't allowed to have my car. So it stayed parked in their driveway for six or nine more months before they finally gave me permission to take it.

Concord House

When I was 18, my parents separated for the thousandth time. But this time felt different. Living with my best friend was great at first but we started bickering about little things and I decided that if we were going to stay friends I needed to move out. My Mom, my brother, and I got our own place. Mom wouldn't tell my dad where our new house was. I really thought she was finally fed up with the years of verbal and physical abuse. I was proud of her, and I told her that. I supported her with many pep talks about how awful Dad was, and she was finally seeing how toxic and manipulating he was. I wanted her to be independent and she was for a minute.

I was determined to keep my family split up this time. But at the same time I was also a teenage girl with distracted parents. I took full advantage, staying out all hours of the night and partying with my friends. Dropping out of high school should have been the biggest red flag to my parents, but they did nothing about it. So, I just tried to have as much fun as possible to forget about my broken home. I felt invisible but I liked it.

My group of friends liked to sit at the old IGA grocery store parking lot and just "bullshit". A few of us girls would walk around town and have "pop machine talks" as we called it, gossiping or venting whatever we needed to do away from the guys. I never talked about my issues with my parents though.

On a random Tuesday or Wednesday night I didn't come home until I saw people heading to work. As I was pulling into the driveway, Mom was warming up her car to leave for the day. She was so mad at me for staying out until 5 a.m. She told me to go inside and go to bed. When she got home that afternoon, she told me that I better never meet her at the door like that again. I had to be home before the sun came up.

So, the next time I stayed out that late, I just waited until she had already left and arrived home at 6 or 7 a.m. to avoid any fighting.

The night that I came home just after midnight and saw an unfamiliar truck in the driveway. I parked and quietly went inside. I

assumed my brother had just gotten another

vehicle. It was there at the door I saw a pair of

old work boots. I recognized these boots. I

walked down the hall to my mother's bedroom

door and cracked it open, my father's familiar

smell smacked me in the face. It was cigarette

smoke and after shave.

I was furious! *What the hell is he doing*

here? I thought to myself. I shut the door and

headed straight for the kitchen, as I opened the

refrigerator there was a 12-pack of his favorite

beer: Miller Genuine Draft on the top shelf. I

took the cans out of the fridge, cracked each

one open, and poured them all down the drain. I

knew he would be pissed but I wanted him to

know that his beer was not welcome in our new

house. I threw the cans in the garbage, went to

my room, and locked the door.

When I woke up the next morning, Dad was gone, and Mom had gone to work. I avoided them as much as I could for several days after that, only going home when I knew no one would be there. How could she let him back in? We were finally free! For the first time in my life our house was finally at peace. I was so disappointed.

A few weeks later, my mom sat me down and told me that something was wrong with Dad. He had become very ill while they were separated, and doctors couldn't give him an explanation. After several months of tests and appointments, they diagnosed him with Hepatitis C and cirrhosis of the liver. Apparently, the stress caused by my parent's separation caused Hepatitis C to flare up. Dad claimed that he must have contracted it through the Marine Corp when he enlisted, but realistically he grew up in the 60s and 70s and he liked to party.

Then Mom explained that deep down she loved Dad, and she was going to take him back so he could have health insurance to help fight his disease. At this time in 2004/2005, there was no cure for Hepatitis C, so all they could do was treat his symptoms as they surfaced.

So, Dad was back. Even though he was sick, I was still pissed and extremely hurt that we were still stuck with him. We left for a reason, and I was so confused that we were just supposed to sweep it under the rug and forget about all the abuse.

Shortly after that, I moved into my

boyfriend's house. Life with him was much better. I quickly became close to his family. I felt closer to them than my own blood. They showed kindness to me and cared about me. Dan encouraged me to finish high school. I spent a few months taking adult ed classes at the library and took the GED test to earn my diploma two months before I would have graduated high school. I can't even tell you how it felt to accomplish that. It felt like I climbed a mountain and then knocked it over.

2007

Sometime between the ages of 21 to 22, I was having car trouble again. I didn't have enough money to pay for rent that month and pay to get my car fixed. So, I had to swallow my pride and ask my parents if I could move home. They had moved from the concord house to a large cabin in the woods.

The cabin was a rental with a full basement: the basement even had its own entry door and full bath. So, I could just come and go without even seeing my family if I wanted. They agreed to let me come home if I paid rent and chipped in on the electric bill. "Okay, sure - I can do that after I fix my car," I promised.

UGLY DUCKLING

My brother who is two years older than me was still living at home, he had never left, and they weren't making him pay any rent. I made sure everyone in the house knew I was pissed about that. I have always felt like I was treated tougher or different than my brothers.

I was the youngest of five kids. My parents each had children when they met. My two oldest half-brothers lived with their mothers and my middle brother lived with my maternal grandparents (are you still with me?). Oldest to youngest siblings: Joe, Dustin, Sean, Anthony and then me.

I don't have a single photograph of all my siblings and me together. We never all lived together at the same time and that bothered me a lot. I felt like I was missing out. I finally told myself that my parents treated me differently because I was the most responsible. The boys each had their own issues but not me. I was the only normal one, so I got the least amount of attention or help.

I came home late on the night of January 17, 2007. I went upstairs to get a snack to take back with me to the basement and my mom was awake. She always went to bed very early because of her work schedule. She startled me.

"What are you doing awake?" I asked her.

She looked at me and I could tell she had been crying. "Dustin died" was all she said.

I was in instant shock. "Wait, what? That can't be!"

I regret thinking it, but my next thought was that he committed suicide. I knew my brother struggled with depression and he was having a rough time.

"He did this to himself, didn't he?" I asked

Mom. She assured me that it was accidental.

He had been struggling since finding out he

was diabetic and wasn't managing his blood

sugar well. He was alone in his truck and

slipped into a diabetic coma.

My brother was dead. I was a wreck. I

wanted to get drunk and feel numb. My dad

didn't handle it well either. He was sick dealing

with Hep C and cirrhosis of the liver. I

remember he stayed in bed and cried for days.

We all did. It was so sad, losing a sibling and

not even getting to say goodbye or I love you.

One month and one day later, on

February 18th, 2007, my dad died of a massive

heart attack in the coffee aisle at Walmart.

When my brother phoned me, he said Dad

collapsed at Walmart and they were taking him by ambulance to the nearby hospital.

Dan and I beat the ambulance to the hospital, and they placed us in a tiny waiting room just off the emergency department. *How could we beat them here?* I thought to myself. A nurse brought my mom and brother into the same waiting room a few minutes after us.

A doctor came in wearing a crisp clean white coat just like you see on television. I jumped up and said, "I want to see my dad, where is he?" He said they were getting dad cleaned up so we could see him, but that he was gone. The EMTs worked on him for over 30 minutes but they couldn't bring him back. They determined later that his heart exploded.

I had a tough relationship with my dad, but I always saw him as invincible. I wished him dead so many times when he was yelling and hitting me but now, he was really gone, and I was shook. It was then that I realized he was the glue holding our family together. It may have been by a trauma bond, but it was never the same after that. Holidays felt like something was missing.

My drinking and partying picked up after that. My heart felt empty and heavy at the same time. In two short months I had lost one of my brothers and my dad. I've heard that time heals all wounds but not something like this.

You just learn to live with the emptiness. For the longest time I made up a story in my head that Dad faked his own death and was still out there somewhere living his life. Whenever I'm in a crowd, I scan the faces hoping to see him but knowing that I won't find him.

After the hospital staff let us see Dad, I sat with his body for a little while alone. His hand was starting to feel cold and all I could think about was the last thing he said to me the day before.

I was loading up my car to run to town and he stopped me outside and said, "Be careful."

"I'm always careful," I answered.

Dad smiled and said, "well, I worry about you cuz I love you."

I waved it off with a smile and left.

That was the last time I saw my dad alive.

My Mother

When I was younger, I used to joke about writing this book. In my mind, it was going to be all about my dad and how his behavior and treatment shaped the way I am. But now that I'm older and actually getting this writing out, I can't ignore the fact that my mom isn't completely innocent.

I see a lot of contributions that I didn't see before. It didn't come to light until after I became a mother myself and constantly thought

How could she do and say these things to me?

I'm her child.

A mother's love is supposed to be unconditional. A mother is the first person you bond with. But what happens when there is no bond? What if you only feel an obligation to keep her in your life? You're a people-pleaser so you try to fix her.

I do remember feeling happiness when I thought of my mom. She was so beautiful, and I wanted to do anything to protect her from my dad. But I also remember "being in her way" in the kitchen. All I wanted was to learn to cook and be near her. But she would never teach me, always telling me to go play instead. I internalized that as I was damaged or unteachable. I hate cooking to this day, and it gives me anxiety because I don't feel good at it.

But I try for my kids, and I get them involved as I learn how to cook myself. Slowly building confidence as I learn from Pinterest and Google. Trying to teach myself that messing up isn't failure, it's learning.

The first time she broke my heart was after my dad passed away. Dad showed us love through money. There were several times dad would give me money as a teen when I was having a bad day. The time when my boyfriend dumped me, he gave me cash to get my hair done, hoping that would make me feel better. He would always say "when I'm gone, you'll get some insurance money. It won't be a lot but it's something to remember me by."

A few months after dad's sudden death my car started acting up. Dan said it would cost a lot to fix it and my car wasn't worth that much. When I approached Mom about receiving my share of Dad's insurance money the first words out of her mouth were "What money? He never said that to me!"

I was shocked and devastated then pissed off. The only words I could form was "HUH?!" I couldn't believe she said that and didn't want to help me. I had to basically beg her and wear her down before she agreed to give me enough money to buy a decent used car. But she was giving both of my brothers' money and had purchased several junkie cars for my brother Anthony during that time. Why did she put up such a fight to keep the money from me? I'll never understand.

Mom received $60k from my dad's insurance policy and I desperately needed $2k for a used car. After Dan pleaded with her and convinced her that the used car in question was a good car, she agreed but only cut me a check for the exact amount. I never saw any more money from her, but over the years my older brothers have milked her for thousands of dollars.

I have come to realize that my mother has a pattern of holding damaged men up on a pedestal and repeatedly treats me like I'm not as important. I have always felt that I was more responsible and level-headed than my brothers and that was the reason my parents didn't show me as much attention or offer me as much help.

Several years later after mom remarried, her husband was battling his siblings over insurance money from the death of his elderly mother. They didn't want to share any of it with her husband. Me being me, I made a comment about how she did that to me too,

once upon a time. She was in complete denial

and claimed to not remember any of that. That

interaction brought all that pain back up again.

It was such a painful and significant moment in

my life and my mother was denying it.

It wasn't until my thirties that I learned

it was okay to start setting boundaries with her.

I had to, to protect my peace. I have noticed she

has become more negative the older she gets.

Our phone conversations only last about five

minutes before I must cut her off to keep her

from bringing down my mood. I want my kids

to form their own opinion of her, but I also

don't want them exposed to her toxic behavior.

When she says to them "Give me a hug

or you can't leave" or "You better hug me, or

I'll spank your butt!" I interrupt her and tell her

she can't talk to my kids like that. She responds with "oh they know I'm just teasing!" No Mom, they don't - they are five and two. When I point out her toxic and abusive behavior, she gets defensive and it usually ends in silent treatment.

We go through phases where I don't speak to her for weeks or even months. I don't know if I will actually go full no contact with her, but I know that would probably be best for me and my family. I really wish she would change and give me the love and support I have always needed but she is almost to retirement age, and I don't see it happening. I now know that the person I have been waiting to rescue me has always been myself.

As I write this book we are not speaking. I decided on New Year's Eve of 2022 that I was fed up with her treatment and negative attitude. It has been several weeks, and the contact has been minimal. I told her not to call me, she could only text. She has texted a few times wanting to see my children. "I miss them," she texted. Not once: "I'm sorry, my daughter. Can we talk?"

I haven't seen her in almost a month, and she ran into my husband today, all weepy-eyed. He told my mom: "Rachel doesn't want to talk to you because you are too negative."

(I'm so proud of him for standing up for me. Even in my late thirties, I'm not used to people doing nice things for me. It makes me feel some type of way).

Her response was: "well I didn't mean to sound negative! She is just like her father!"

So here we are. Instead of accepting

fault and apologizing, my mother is placing the blame on my dead father.

Being involved in my children's life is a privilege. I have closed the door on long-term friendships because my children are more important. I will do the same with any family member in the blink of an eye. I refuse to let her shade them with her toxic treatment.

It's not fair that I must constantly fight for my peace from her. I get so jealous when I see women my age or younger that have great relationships with their mom and they do fun things together, or when I see grandparents pick up their grandkids for the weekend for no reason at all.

I could have a relationship with her if I were fake and pretended like everything was fine. But I can't make myself do it. I've never been a fake person and as I get older, I am very blunt with my feelings and I'm brutally honest.

My advice to you is this: if you are dealing with anyone in your life that is causing you pain or difficulty, stand up for yourself. You must look out for yourself, and your mental health. Don't let people treat you badly just because you share DNA. If you don't get excited to see or speak to them, then that is a red flag. You need to listen to your gut to protect your peace.

30s Are for Healing

Inside myself, I didn't feel like I deserved to be a mother. I grew up yearning for love and it only damaged me. Could I love a child? Would I be a good mother? Would the generational trauma continue onto my children? How do I explain my messed-up family?

One day it just clicked. It was like a switch flipped in my brain. I would constantly ask myself *am I missing out? Am I good enough to raise a child? What if I screw them up?* Wondering if I was destined to be just like my parents. If I did agree to have kids, I would do everything possible to raise them with unconditional love and understanding. If I were to bring a child into the world, they wouldn't owe me anything. My parents always acted like I always owed them something just for existing.

I finally decided one night over a few drinks to talk to my husband about our no-kids decision. I asked if he felt like we were missing out and he said "maybe" and then the universe kept giving us sign after sign that we couldn't ignore. By now Dan and I had been together for 13 years, everyone had finally stopped asking the intrusive "when are you having kids" questions.

The night Dan's grandpa died was when we finally decided. November 3rd, 2016, was the night that the Chicago Cubs won the world series. We watched it on the television at the VA hospital as we sat with Grandpa waiting for him to take his last breath. Shortly after the Cubs won, and he took his last breath. We were all in tears.

We left the hospital at 1 or 2 a.m. On our drive home I said, "we need to have babies and live on the farm." Dan agreed, and that was that.

I gave birth to our first son in December 2017. We moved into our new house built on five acres of his grandpa's land the summer of 2018 and our second son was born in August 2020. I'm so happy we changed our mind. There is nothing like the love you feel for your child. As soon as Lincoln was born and he looked up at me, it was this instant connection. I felt like he was looking into my soul. I have never felt anything like that before until my second son was born. It is love at first sight and more. An invisible string from my soul to my child's.

After the birth of my first son Lincoln, something in me changed. I learned that if you experience trauma as a child that you are more susceptible to postpartum depression. I had no idea. It hit me like a ton of bricks; I couldn't relax, I was constantly on edge. Loud noises set me off and I felt so much rage.

I would sleep at night with my eyeglasses in my hand so I could get up quickly when the baby started to cry. I would get out of bed several times a night to check that he was still breathing and then I would lay there and play the worst-case scenario game in my head. I thought for sure that something awful would happen to Lincoln's because he was just too perfect.

It was very lonely. I felt like I was drowning and didn't know how to explain what I was feeling. I thought postpartum depression was feeling suicidal or thoughts about hurting your newborn. I was anxious and angry. I just kept telling myself that it was just from sleep deprivation, and it was normal.

For the longest time I was on autopilot during the day. I was terrified of the nighttime when the anxiety would hit and I couldn't sleep. I tried CBD oil, essential oils, nothing was helping. So, I just sucked it up because I thought getting on medication for a doctor meant I failed. That I wasn't tough enough to handle my new role.

The laundry set me off one day. I

wanted to do a task that didn't involve

breastfeeding or changing a baby. When I

heard the washer beep, I jumped up. I was

actually excited to switch the laundry out. I

opened the washer and started to grab the wet

clothes. As I opened the dry door, it was still

full of clean clothes. I slammed the door and

started cussing. The cussing turned into crying

and screaming. I felt insane at that moment, but

I couldn't stop what was happening to me. Dan

came in and told me to go lay down. He knew

that something wasn't right with me, but he

didn't know how to help me. We were like two

ships passing in the night.

　　While Dan was building our house, we

were living in my mom's spare room. We

would take turns sleeping out in the living

room with Lincoln and the other one would be

able to rest in the bedroom.

When Lincoln turned one, I finally had the courage to get help. After I described how I was feeling and what I had been going through, the doctor looked at me and said "Rachel, you have postpartum depression and anxiety."
I laughed at him and said, "I'm not depressed."
He wrote me a prescription.

Three days into taking my antidepressants, I woke up happy. I felt so much lighter, and I started crying. I finally admitted to myself how miserable I had been for the last 12 months.

I regret waiting a year to get help. I can be so damn stubborn sometimes and I'm very lucky that I didn't lose myself completely during that time. After I started taking care of my mental health, I began to notice the toxic

110

advice I kept hearing.

My mother's advice also came as I navigated my way through my new role as a mother. I remember her saying "don't hold him too much, you'll spoil him. You should let him cry it out, that's the only way he'll learn to soothe himself."

Every time she would give advice my body would cringe. It just didn't feel right to me. Instead of listening to her advice I just did what felt right. If he cried, I went to him. I nursed him to sleep. He needed contact to rest well, so I would hold him for all his naps. At the time I would get frustrated because I felt like I needed to be up doing chores or other things. Looking back, I was right where I was supposed to be.

Eventually after I got to know and bond

with Lincoln, I could tell what he needed by the sound of his cry. When I became a mother, I also started realizing how damaged my inner child was. I started waking up every day with one goal: to be what I needed at his age.

The triggers didn't start happening until we went from one kid to two. At times it would get a little chaotic and make me very anxious. Your 2.5-year-old needs you, but the newborn is crying - or you're trying to get the newborn to sleep but your toddler is being loud. It was a huge adjustment for all of us, and it made me a nervous wreck.

On top of that, Henry had Torticollis and colic shortly after birth and we had no idea why he was so cranky. The lactation consultant at our pediatrician's office was the one that

112

pointed it out. I had never heard of Torticollis before, but it has to do with the muscles in the neck being constricted and the head tilts one direction.

We started taking Henry to a pediatric chiropractor and after a few adjustments his neck pain was decreasing. But his colic hung around until he was about 3 months old.

It was hard on my mental health. His screaming would make my entire body tense and I would start to panic. I loved my baby, but I didn't like him very much for the first year of his life.

Fast forward now Henry is a very happy 2.5-year-old. The boys get quite loud when they are playing and that triggers me. When the kids start fighting, that triggers me.

There was an instance where Lincoln

was playing with Dan's belt, and he taught Lincoln how to snap it. That instantly triggered me and sent me into a panic attack. I was shaking and had to go outside to calm down. My dad wore a leather belt and when he would threaten my brother or myself, he would snap the belt as a warning. Just thinking about it makes me tense up.

I'm now 38 years old, and I'm trying to teach myself how to regulate my own emotions so I can teach those skills to my children.

There are some days when I get overstimulated and triggered and I feel so much guilt for getting set off by the kids. I'm unlearning every day and I'm so hard on myself. I know I can't be perfect, but I want to be perfect for them. I am trying not to yell at them or instantly want to spank them when I get set off. I don't want to raise my kids that way because I hated that as a child.

Healing myself while raising two tiny humans is by far the hardest thing I've ever done. But I'm learning to accept that I'm not perfect and it's okay to mess up. I have occasional pep talks with myself when I remind myself that there is a reason why it's hard at times: I'm the chosen one to end the generational trauma of fear-based parenting. I will be the cycle breaker. This toxic, abusive behavior will end with me.

In this house there is no abuse, just a whole lot of love. I love when my five year old son runs up to me for no reason and says "Mommy I love you, I'm so happy" it literally makes my eyes fill with tears and my heart melt. I absolutely love being the mom of two crazy little boys. They are free to be themselves. I'm their comfort. It makes my heart swell when they are scared or upset, and they just need me to hold them.

Lincoln crawls into our bed a lot at night because he gets scared. I don't mind it one bit. I know it won't be like this for long, as Darius Rucker says. I never felt comfortable enough to crawl in my parents' bed. The fact that I'm his safe person makes me feel like Wonder Woman. I look forward to watching them grow and do great things in this world. As they grow, my inner child heals and grows with them. I just hope my trauma doesn't turn into their trauma and that my kids don't grow up hating me. I hope they know that I'll always be there for them no matter what. Now when I look back on my childhood, my only thought is

UGLY DUCKLING

- I can endure a lot, but does that mean I must?

"We'll see if one tree won't grow as crooked as
another, with the same wind to twist it!" –
Heathcliff, *Wuthering Heights*

About the Author

Rachel Weddle grew up in a small town in South Central Indiana. She is now a full time stay at home mother and part time writer. In her free time, she likes to practice yoga, enjoys painting, reading, and listening to true crime podcasts. After living away from her hometown for almost a decade, she and her husband moved back to their hometown and now live with their two children on a five-acre farm in the countryside.

Made in the USA
Monee, IL
28 June 2023

37922498R00068